The MAILBOX®

The Education Center®

grade **2**

Daily Math Prompts

One math prompt for every day of the school year!

- ### Review key math skills.

- ### Engage students in writing about math.

- ### Promote students' mathematical thinking.

Written by Ann Hefflin

Managing Editor: Gerri Primak

Editorial Team: Becky S. Andrews, Kimberley Bruck, Sharon Murphy, Debra Liverman, Diane Badden, Thad H. McLaurin, Kelly Robertson, Karen A. Brudnak, Jennifer Nunn, Hope Rodgers, Dorothy C. McKinney

Production Team: Lori Z. Henry, Pam Crane, Rebecca Saunders, Chris Curry, Sarah Foreman, Theresa Lewis Goode, Greg D. Rieves, Eliseo De Jesus Santos II, Barry Slate, Donna K. Teal, Zane Williard, Tazmen Carlisle, Kathy Coop, Marsha Heim, Lynette Dickerson, Mark Rainey, Laurel Robinson

www.themailbox.com

©2007 The Mailbox®
All rights reserved.
ISBN10 #1-56234-772-1 • ISBN13 #978-156234-772-7

Manufactured in the United States
10 9 8 7 6 5 4 3 2 1

Table of Contents

How to Use This Book

Select a Prompt

To support your math curriculum, the prompts are arranged sequentially from easier to harder skills. Begin with the first page of prompts and work your way to the last page, or use the skills grid on page 4 to help you choose prompts that best suit the needs of your students. The handy checklist on page 77 will help you keep track of the prompts you've used throughout the year.

Display the Prompt

Prompts can be displayed in many ways. Here are a few suggestions:

● Photocopy selected prompts and cut them into strips. Give one copy of a selected strip to each student.

● Make copies of a page of prompts and give one to each student at the beginning of the week.

● Copy the prompt onto the board or on a piece of chart paper to display in the classroom or at a center.

● Make a transparency of the prompts to show on an overhead projector.

● If a visual is not needed, read the prompt aloud to students.

Additional Ways to Use This Book

- Use math prompts as
  - morning work
  - independent work
  - homework
  - a warm-up activity
  - a small-group activity

- Create individual student math journals by stapling a copy of the math journal cover (page 79) atop a supply of notebook paper. Or, if desired, use copies of the journal pages (page 80) instead of notebook paper. Math journals are a great way to keep a record of students' mathematical thinking and writing.

- Take a quick assessment of your students' mathematical thinking by using the assessment forms on page 78.

- Talk with individual students about their prompts to get a deeper insight into their mathematical thinking.

Skills Grid

Skill	Prompt
NUMBER AND OPERATIONS	
Number Sense	
comparing numbers	41, 68, 73
estimation	37, 62
mathematical thinking	51, 58, 82
number order	6, 11, 32, 77, 92, 173
odd and even numbers	16, 67
ordinal numbers	18
place value	1, 23, 26, 27, 52, 56, 96, 172
problem solving	178
Addition and Subtraction	
addition	2, 12, 17, 46, 61, 72, 91, 97
addition and subtraction	8, 63, 87
addition story problems	22, 28, 36, 42, 48, 57, 66, 83, 101, 112, 137
addition with regrouping	31
strategies	33, 38, 102
subtraction	13, 76, 81, 93, 106, 113, 117
subtraction story problems	3, 21, 43, 47, 53, 71, 78, 86, 98, 108
subtraction with regrouping	133
Money	
adding and subtracting money	146
adding money	118, 142, 151
coin value	107, 121
comparing values	122, 138
money combinations	88, 103, 111, 126, 131, 136, 141, 148
subtracting money	116, 161
Multiplication and Division	
array	128
basic multiplication	132, 137, 157, 162, 166, 176
understanding division	127, 171, 177
Fractions	
parts of a set	153, 156, 158, 163, 167
parts of a whole	7, 123, 143, 147, 152, 168
GEOMETRY	
comparing plane and solid figures	70, 155
congruency	94, 120
plane figures	10, 14, 25, 35, 60, 129, 144
solid figures	110, 135, 165, 179
symmetry	40, 79

Skill	Prompt
MEASUREMENT	
calendar	39
capacity	175
length	95, 114, 125
perimeter	104
temperature	169
time	5, 19, 29, 45, 59, 65, 75, 85, 134
tools	159
weight	149
DATA ANALYSIS & PROBABILITY	
bar graph	50, 55, 74, 84, 90
collecting data	130
comparing graphs	139
pictograph	34, 69
probability	150, 164, 170, 180
table	109
tally chart	9, 20, 90, 99, 115
ALGEBRA	
choosing a number sentence	124
comparing sums	24
finding a rule	54, 145
missing addend	30, 44
missing digits	80
missing factor	140
missing subtrahend	49
number patterns	15, 64, 105, 160
picture patterns	100
problem solving	174
shape patterns	4
using symbols	119
writing number sentences	89, 154

1. Jill says that 2 tens equal 20 ones. Is she right? Tell how you know.

2. How can you use a number line to find the sum of 7 and 5?

3. Tim has 9 apples. He gives 3 away. How many apples does he have left? Use pictures, words, and numbers to show how you know.

4. Copy the pattern. Then draw the next three shapes. How did you know what to draw?

5. Sam begins his homework at 4:00. Look at the clock. Is it time for him to start? Explain.

Answer Key

1. yes

2. Answers will vary.

3. 6 apples

4. △△○

5. no

6. Write these numbers in order from least to greatest: 27, 19, 17. Tell why this order is correct.

7. What fraction of the circle is shaded? Explain what the fraction means.

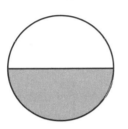

8. Here's one way to show 16. Think of at least three other ways to show 16. Use numbers, pictures, and words to show your answers.

$$4 + 4 + 4 + 4 = 16$$

9. Jim asked each of his classmates to pick a color. Look at the chart. Which color was picked the most? How do you know?

Colors Picked

Color	Tally Marks
blue	|||
green	||
red	‖‖‖ ||
pink	‖‖‖

10. How are a square and a triangle alike? How are they different?

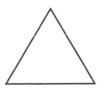

6. 17, 19, 27

7. ½

8. Answers will vary.

9. red

10. Answers will vary.

NUMBER & OPERATIONS

11. Copy and complete the list of numbers. How did you know what the missing numbers were?

14, ___, 16, 17, ___, ___, 20

NUMBER & OPERATIONS

12. Show two different ways Kelly can find the sum of 7 + 8. Explain your thinking.

NUMBER & OPERATIONS

13. David has 18 ride tickets. He gives 11 away to his friends. Write a number sentence to show how many tickets he has left. How did you know whether to add or subtract?

GEOMETRY

14. What is a triangle? Tell how you know using pictures, numbers, and words.

ALGEBRA

15. Sam writes the following list of numbers. If he keeps following the same rule, what will the next three numbers be? How do you know?

6, 9, 12, 15, 18, 21, ___ , ___, ___

11. 14, <u>15</u>, 16, 17, <u>18</u>, <u>19</u>, 20

12. Answers will vary.

13. 18 – 11 = 7 tickets

14. Answers will vary.

15. 24, 27, 30

16. Kim wants to know if 15 is an odd or an even number. Explain how she can figure it out.

17. Use the counting on strategy to solve 38 + 5. Explain what you did.

18. Nina has her crayons in this order: black, brown, red, pink, orange, yellow, green, blue, purple, white. Which color is third? Which color is eighth? Tell how you know.

19. Mike goes to bed every night at 8:00. Is that AM or PM? How do you know?

20. In Mr. Reed's class, 4 students like crackers, 8 students like cookies, 6 students like candy, and 3 students like fruit. Complete a tally chart to display this information. Explain what the chart shows.

Popular Snacks

Snack	Tally Marks
crackers	
cookies	
candy	
fruit	

16. odd

17. 43

18. red, blue

19. PM

20.

Snack	Tally Marks
crackers	IIII
cookies	HHT III
candy	HHT I
fruit	III

NUMBER & OPERATIONS

21. Miss Mack has 18 buttons. She puts 7 on her shirt. How many buttons does she have left? Explain how you solved the problem.

NUMBER & OPERATIONS

22. Jamal bakes 30 cookies for the bake sale. Ryan bakes 50 cookies. How many cookies do they bake in all? How did you get the answer?

NUMBER & OPERATIONS

23. Annie puts her dolls in 5 groups of ten. She has 7 dolls left over. How many dolls does she have? Show how you got your answer.

ALGEBRA

24. Pam solved 12 + 6 and got 18. Jake is solving 6 + 12. He is sure that his sum will be the same. Is he right? How do you know?

GEOMETRY

25. I am a shape. I have four sides. Not all my sides are equal. The sides across from each other are equal. What shape am I?

21. 11 buttons

22. 80 cookies

23. 57 dolls

24. yes

25. rectangle

NUMBER & OPERATIONS

26. Manny has 23 cookies. His cookie bags hold 10 cookies each. How many bags can he fill? How many cookies will be left over? Explain your answers.

NUMBER & OPERATIONS

27. What is the value of 3 in the number 43? How do you know?

NUMBER & OPERATIONS

28. Robby has 25 baseball cards. He has 26 football cards. He wants to know how many cards he has in all. Use numbers, pictures, and words to show two different ways he could figure this out.

MEASUREMENT

29. How many minutes past five o'clock is it? What time is it? Tell how you got your answer.

ALGEBRA

30. Jenny has 13 marbles. She finds some more. Now she has 18 marbles. How many did she find? Explain how you got the answer.

26. 2 bags, 3 cookies

27. 3 ones

28. 51 cards

29. 35 minutes, 5:35

30. 5 marbles

NUMBER & OPERATIONS

31. Amy is adding 34 and 7. Will she need to regroup to find the sum? How do you know?

NUMBER & OPERATIONS

32. Cameron thinks the following numbers are in order from greatest to least. Is she correct? Why or why not?

57, 35, 42, 28

NUMBER & OPERATIONS

33. Pedro says knowing that 7 – 3 = 4 makes it easy to solve 70 – 30. What does he mean?

DATA ANALYSIS & PROBABILITY

34. Look at the pictograph. How many more children like orange juice than grape juice? Explain how you got your answer.

Favorite Juices

Juice	Children
Grape	
Apple	
Orange	

🥤 = 1 child

GEOMETRY

35. Look at the shapes. Tell which two have the same number of sides and corners.

31. yes

32. no

33. Answers will vary.

34. 3 children

35. square and rectangle

NUMBER & OPERATIONS

36. Cole has 43 stickers. A friend gives him 10 more. How many stickers does he have now? Explain how you know.

NUMBER & OPERATIONS

37. Jack has 18 goldfish and 24 angelfish in his fish tank. Estimate how many fish are in the tank in all. Explain how rounding helped you find your answer.

NUMBER & OPERATIONS

38. Look at the subtraction problems. Which one could be best solved by counting back? Which one could be best solved using doubles? Explain your thinking.

14-7   18-3

MEASUREMENT

39. The school principal leaves on a two-week vacation on the first Monday of the month. On what day will she return from her trip? How do you know?

Sun.	Mon.	Tues.	Wed.	Thur.	Fri.	Sat.
		1	2	3	4	5
6	7	8	9	10	11	12
13	14	15	16	17	18	19
20	21	22	23	24	25	26
27	28	29	30	31		

GEOMETRY

40. Write a capital letter A on your paper. Draw a line of symmetry through it. How did you know where to draw the line?

36. 53 stickers

37. Answers will vary.

38. 18 – 3,   14 – 7

39. Monday, the 21st

40. 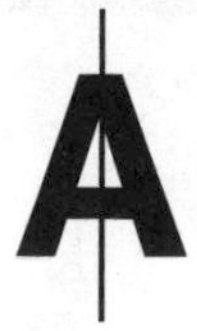 A

41. Is 62 greater than, less than, or equal to 45? Write >, <, or =. How did you know what to write?

62 ◯ 45

42. Sarah caught 26 fish in the morning. She caught 15 more in the afternoon. How many fish did she catch in all? Explain how you got your answer.

43. Simon has 36 pieces of candy. He gives 20 pieces away. How many pieces of candy does he have left? Did you add or subtract to solve the problem? Why?

44. Sue and Tommy sold lemonade. They sold 32 cups of lemonade in all. Sue sold 15 cups. How many cups of lemonade did Tommy sell? Explain how you got your answer.

45. The time is 8:10. How many minutes are there until it is 9:00? How do you know?

41. >

42. 41 fish

43. 16 pieces, subtract

44. 17 cups

45. 50 minutes

NUMBER & OPERATIONS

46. Explain how you can use mental math to solve 53 + 47.

NUMBER & OPERATIONS

47. Greg collected 57 cans. Zach collected 31 cans. How many more cans did Greg collect? Explain how you got your answer.

NUMBER & OPERATIONS

48. Write a story problem using this number sentence. Then solve the problem.

$$36 + 14 = \underline{\quad}$$

ALGEBRA

49. Find the missing number. What did you do to find it?

$$63 - \underline{\quad} = 22$$

DATA ANALYSIS & PROBABILITY

50. The bar graph shows the favorite stickers of the students in Ms. Conroy's class. Which type of sticker did the most students like best? How do you know?

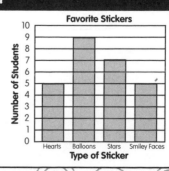

Favorite Stickers

Answer Key

46. Answers will vary.

47. 26 cans

48. 50

49. 41

50. balloons

51. Ethan knows that 32 + 4 is the same as 36. Show other ways you can make 36 using numbers, pictures, and words.

52. What is the value of 8 in the number 481? Tell how you know.

481

53. Fred has 52 brown chickens and 35 white chickens. How many more brown chickens does he have than white chickens? Explain how you got your answer.

54. Find a rule for the table. Then complete the table. How did you find the rule?

In	Out
18	13
16	11
14	
12	

55. Bob asked his friends to name their favorite animals. The answers were dog, cat, pig, dog, dog, pig, cat, frog, dog, frog, pig, and horse. Show Bob how to display the data on a bar graph. Explain the graph's results.

Favorite Animals

Number of People (0–7)

dog cat pig frog horse

Animals

51. Answers will vary.

52. 8 tens

53. 17 more brown chickens

54. subtract 5

In	Out
18	13
16	11
14	9
12	7

55.

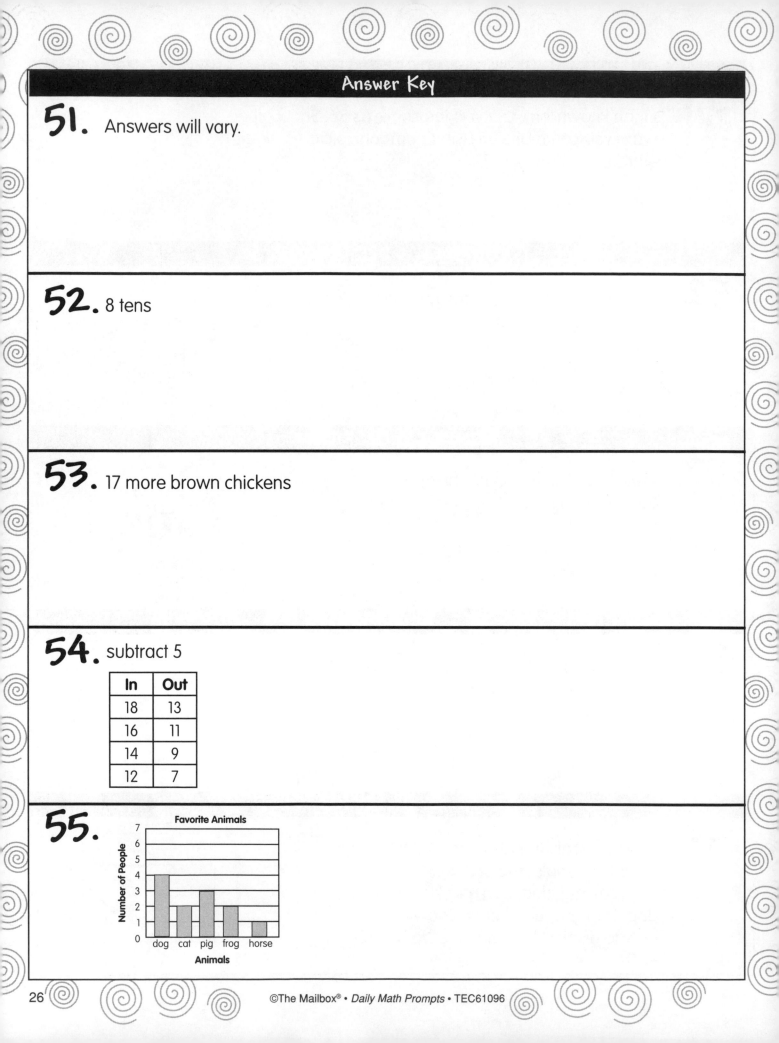

56. Danny says there is a 7 in the tens place of the number 756. Do you agree or disagree with Danny? Why or why not?

57. Shayna made 12 bookmarks. Ted made 6 more bookmarks than Shayna. How many bookmarks did Ted make? How many did they make in all?

58. Read the number. Use pictures, numbers, or words to show the number two other ways.

493

59. Paul's aunt is taking him to the park for a picnic. About how much time will they need: 3 days, 3 minutes, or 3 hours? Explain how you know.

60. Brandon has two triangles. How can he put them together to make a square? Draw the new shape.

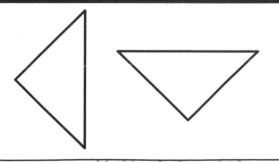

56. disagree

57. 18 bookmarks, 30 bookmarks

58. Answers will vary.

59. 3 hours

60.

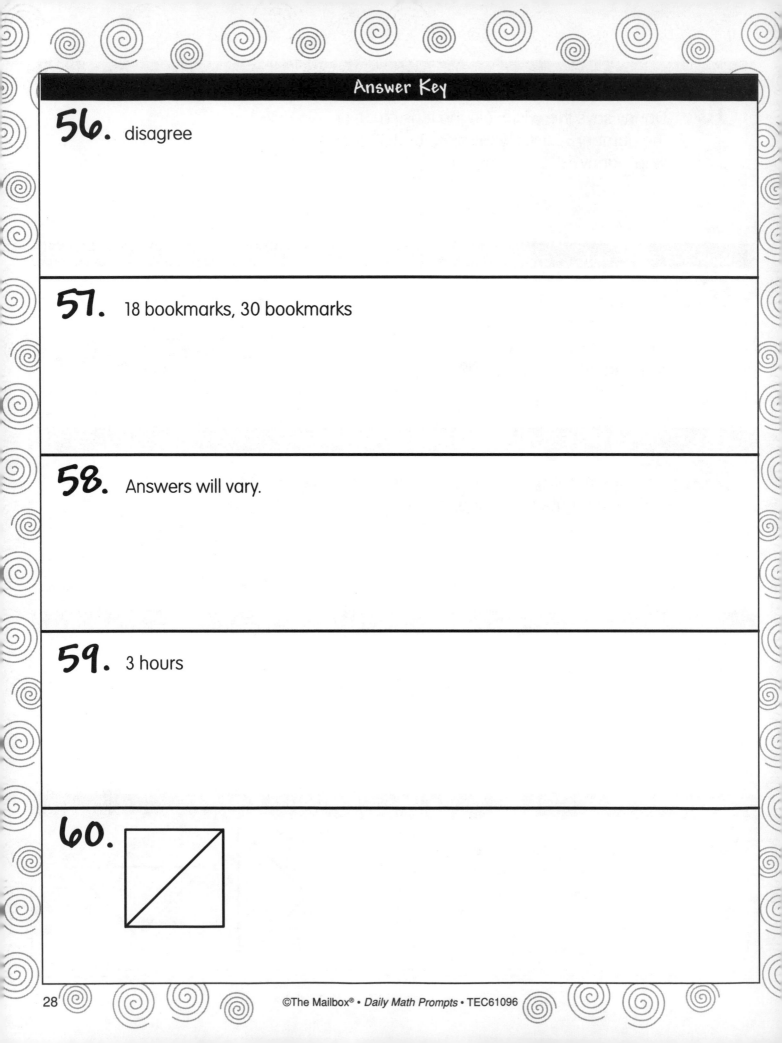

NUMBER & OPERATIONS

61. Choose from the numbers shown to make two different addition problems with the sum of 51. Show how you know you are right.

23   25   26   28

NUMBER & OPERATIONS

62. Marcus read 18 pages of his book. Steve read 32 pages of his book. Estimate how many more pages Steve read than Marcus. Explain how you got your estimate.

NUMBER & OPERATIONS

63. Use addition to check the answer for 55 – 27 = 28. Is the answer correct? Explain how you figured it out.

ALGEBRA

64. What is the rule for the pattern? How do you know you are right? Complete the pattern.

340, 360, 380, 400, ___, ___, ___

MEASUREMENT

65. A baseball game starts at 1:00 and ends at 4:00. How long does it last? Explain how you got your answer.

61. 23 + 28 = 51 or 28 + 23 and 25 + 26 = 51 or 26 + 25

62. about 10 more pages

63. yes

64. add 20; 420, 440, 460

65. 3 hours

66. Adam makes a house with 25 blocks. Then he adds 7 more. Albert makes a house with 41 blocks. How many blocks did they use in all? Explain how you got your answer.

67. Is 46 an odd or even number? How do you know?

68. Write two numbers that are greater than 375. Tell how you know you are right.

69. Look at the pictograph. How many more chocolate chip cookies were sold than oatmeal-raisin cookies? Explain how you got your answer.

Cookie Sale

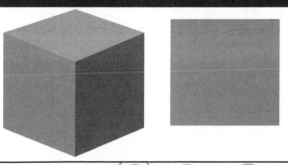

Kind of Cookie	
oatmeal raisin	🍪🍪
chocolate chip	🍪🍪🍪🍪🍪
peanut butter	🍪🍪🍪
sugar	🍪🍪🍪🍪

🍪 = 2 cookies

70. Name the two figures. How are they alike? How are they different? Explain.

66. 73 blocks

67. even

68. Answers will vary.

69. 8 more chocolate chip cookies

70. cube and square

NUMBER & OPERATIONS

71. Cindy has 24 crackers. She gives 15 crackers to her friend. How many crackers does Cindy have left? Explain how you solved the problem.

NUMBER & OPERATIONS

72. What is the sum of 30 and 18? Write your answer in both number and word form. How did you get your answer?

NUMBER & OPERATIONS

73. Write two numbers that are less than 266. Tell how you know you are right.

DATA ANALYSIS & PROBABILITY

74. Katie counted the number of flowers of each color in her garden. Look at the table. Use its data to create a bar graph. Explain the graph's results.

Color	Number of Flowers
red	5
blue	6
purple	8
white	3

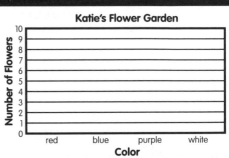

MEASUREMENT

75. Jan says that it is 25 minutes after three o'clock. Is she right? Why or why not?

71. 9 crackers

72. 48, forty-eight

73. Answers will vary.

74.

Katie's Flower Garden

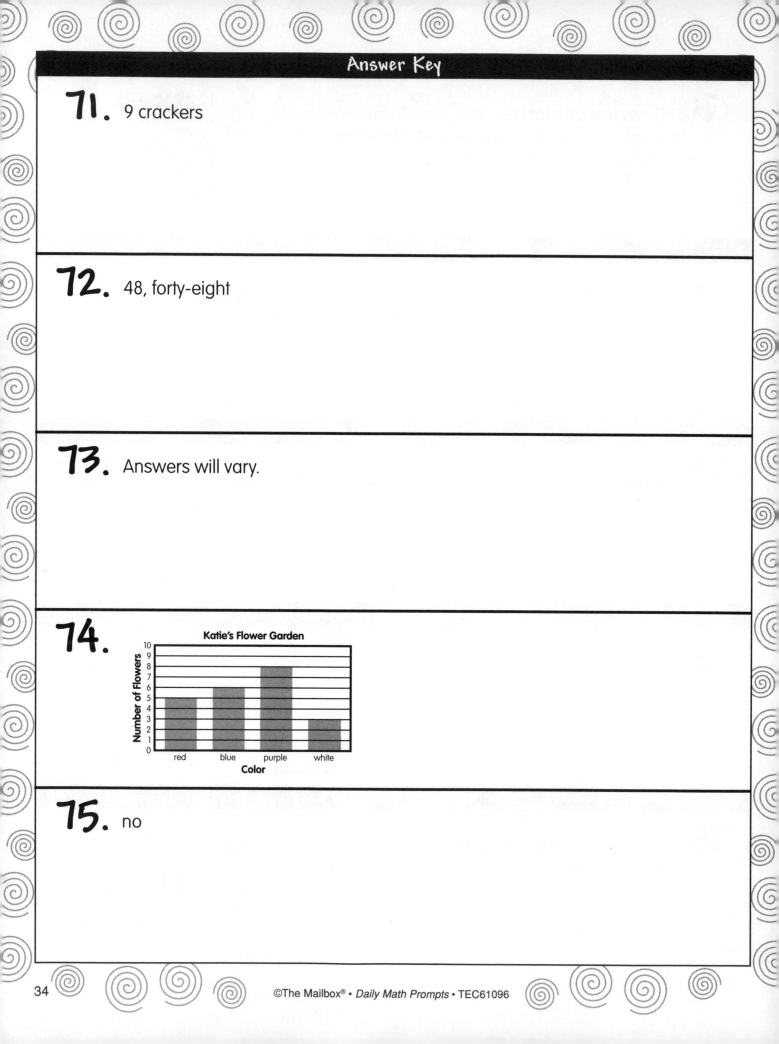

75. no

NUMBER & OPERATIONS

76. Chen asks you to help him solve 23 – 6 using base-ten blocks. Use numbers, pictures, and words to show him how to solve the problem in this way.

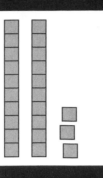

NUMBER & OPERATIONS

77. Order these numbers from least to greatest. Tell why this order is correct.

596, 536, 563, 559, 593

NUMBER & OPERATIONS

78. Devin picks 75 apples. He gives 25 to his friend. Then he gives 23 to his teacher. How many apples does Devin have left? Explain what you did to solve the problem.

GEOMETRY

79. Which picture shows a line of symmetry? Tell how you know.

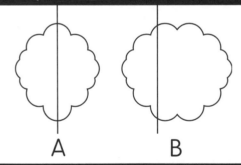

A   B

ALGEBRA

80. Identify the missing digits in the problem. Explain how you got your answers.

$$\begin{array}{r} 6\square \\ -\ \square4 \\ \hline 51 \end{array}$$

76. Answers will vary.

77. 536, 559, 563, 593, 596

78. 27 apples

79. picture A

80.
```
  6 [5]
- [1] 4
─────
  5 1
```

81. Look at the problem. Which of the following answers makes the most sense: 7, 17, or 27? Explain your answer; then solve the problem to check your work.

$$35 - 18$$

82. Write this number in two different ways. Use pictures, numbers, and words to show your work.

293

83. Kristen has 70 beads. She gets 40 more. How many beads does she have in all? How did you get your answer?

84. Look at the graph. Altogether, how many kids liked soccer, baseball, or football? How did you use the graph to find your answer?

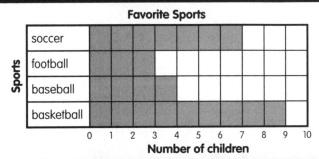

Favorite Sports

Sports: soccer, football, baseball, basketball
Number of children: 0 1 2 3 4 5 6 7 8 9 10

85. Avi has baseball practice two hours after his piano lesson. His piano lesson is three hours after his swimming lesson. If his piano lesson is at 4:00, at what times are his swimming lesson and baseball practice? Explain how you got your answer.

81. 17

82. Answers will vary.

83. 110 beads

84. 14 kids

85. 1:00 and 6:00

NUMBER & OPERATIONS

86. Carlos has 100 fewer baseball cards than Ricky. If Ricky has 585 baseball cards, how many baseball cards does Carlos have? Show how you got your answer. Then explain your work.

John Swingalot

NUMBER & OPERATIONS

87. Use addition to check the answer for the following problem. Show your work.

$$65 - 37 = 28$$

NUMBER & OPERATIONS

88. Ravi needs 65 cents to ride the train at the park. He has 1 quarter, 2 dimes, 2 nickels, and 8 pennies. Does he have enough money? Explain how you got your answer.

ALGEBRA

89. Use the following numbers to write three different number sentences. Explain your answers.

82   49   33

DATA ANALYSIS & PROBABILITY

90. Tina used the tally chart to create a graph about her friends' favorite pet choices. Is her graph correct? Why or why not?

Favorite Pets

Pet	Tally Marks
fish	II
dog	HHT HHT
cat	HHT II
bird	III

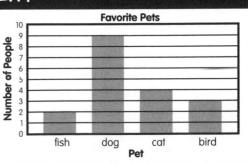

86. 485 baseball cards

87. Answers will vary.

88. no

89. Answers will vary.

90. no

NUMBER & OPERATIONS

91. Look at the following numbers. Choose two numbers that can be added together without regrouping. Solve the problem to show that your choices are correct.

199   462

235   656

NUMBER & OPERATIONS

92. Dre is thinking of two numbers. One is just before 672, and one is just after 672. What two numbers is he thinking of? Explain how you know.

NUMBER & OPERATIONS

93. Lucy and Carrie are solving the same problem. Lucy wants to count back to find the answer. Carrie wants to regroup. Solve the problem both ways to show the girls how both will work.

45 – 6

GEOMETRY

94. Which two shapes are congruent? Explain how you know.

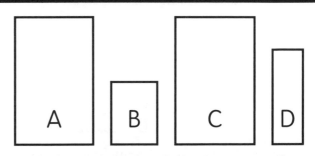

MEASUREMENT

95. Devon says that his pencil is six inches long. Is he right? Why or why not?

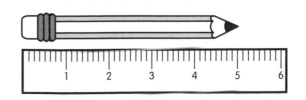

91. 235 and 462; 697

92. 671 and 673

93. 39

94.

A	C

95. no

NUMBER & OPERATIONS

96. I am a three-digit number. My hundreds digit is a 9. My tens digit is 5 less than my hundreds digit. My ones digit is the same as my tens digit. What number am I?

_____ _____ _____

NUMBER & OPERATIONS

97. To add 267 and 325, do you have to regroup? Tell how you know.

NUMBER & OPERATIONS

98. There are 216 players at soccer camp. There are 128 soccer balls for practice. How many more players are there than balls? Explain how you got your answer.

DATA ANALYSIS & PROBABILITY

99. Lana asked her classmates what their favorite milk shake flavors are. Use the information she recorded in the table to create a graph to display her data. Explain what the graph shows.

Milk Shake Flavor	Number of Students
chocolate	卌 卌
vanilla	卌 III
strawberry	IIII
peanut butter	卌 I

ALGEBRA

100. Look at the circles. Is there a pattern? Why or why not?

96. 944

97. yes

98. 88 more soccer players

99. Graphs will vary.

100. no

NUMBER & OPERATIONS

101. Mandy has 172 bows. Sasha has 150 bows. Write a number sentence to figure out how many bows they have in all. Did you add or subtract? Why?

NUMBER & OPERATIONS

102. Explain how knowing the answer to 9 – 5 helps you solve 900 – 500.

NUMBER & OPERATIONS

103. Rich is buying a cookie for 47 cents. Draw the coins he could use. How did you know what to draw?

MEASUREMENT

104. What is the perimeter of this square? Explain how you got your answer.

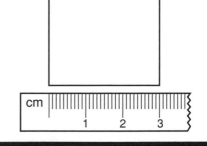

ALGEBRA

105. The rule is subtract 5. The starting number is 55. Write the next five numbers in the pattern. How do you know your pattern is right?

55, ____, ____, ____, ____, ____

101. 172 + 150 = 322, add

102. Answers will vary.

103. Answers will vary.

104. 12 cm

105. 50, 45, 40, 35, 30

NUMBER & OPERATIONS

106. Jess subtracted to find a difference of 59. Which of the following could be the other two numbers in the problem? Show how you got your answer.

245, 128, 186, 342

NUMBER & OPERATIONS

107. Put these coins in order from the largest value to the smallest value. What is the total amount of money? Explain how you know.

NUMBER & OPERATIONS

108. Melissa sold 389 cupcakes at the bake sale last week. LaToya sold 345 cupcakes. How many more cupcakes did Melissa sell than LaToya? Show your work. Explain what you did.

DATA ANALYSIS & PROBABILITY

109. This table shows Mr. Booker's students' favorite pie flavors. Using the information in the table, tell which two pie flavors he should buy for a class treat. Explain your choices.

Favorite Pie Flavors

Pie Flavor	Number of Students
cherry	3
apple	9
peach	3
pumpkin	8

GEOMETRY

110. Sort the following figures into two groups. Describe each group and explain why each figure belongs in it.

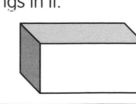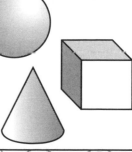

106. 245 and 186

107. 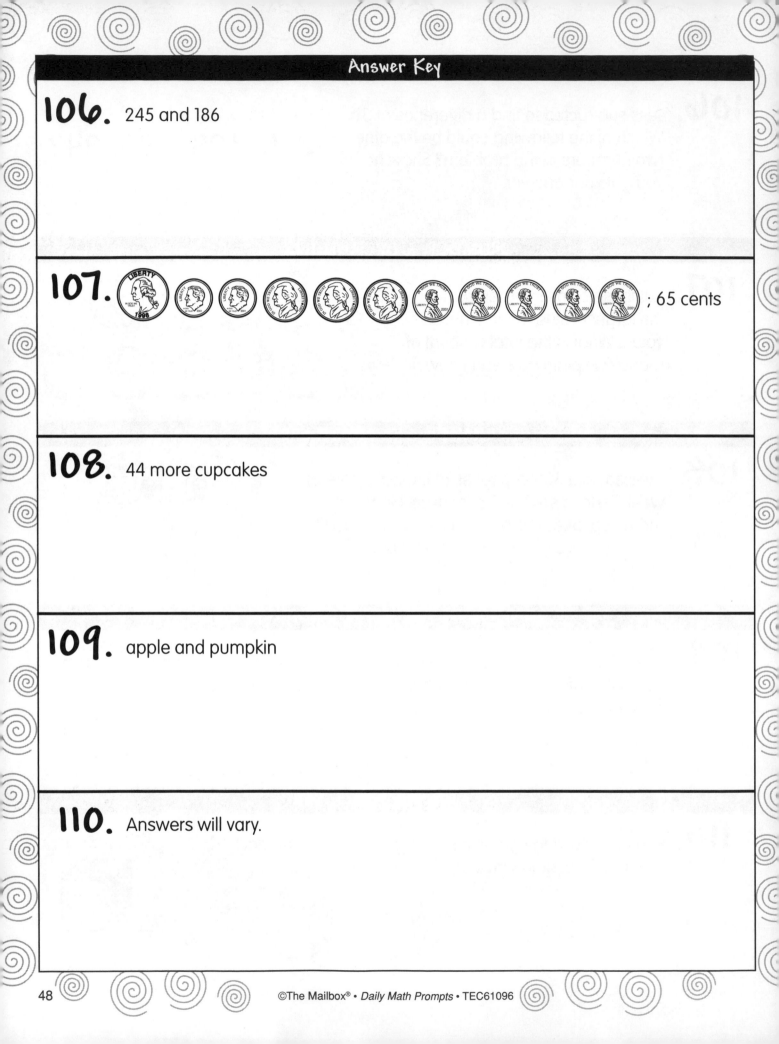 ; 65 cents

108. 44 more cupcakes

109. apple and pumpkin

110. Answers will vary.

111. Draw three coins that equal 55 cents. How do you know that your drawing is right?

112. Luke has 245 books. Jake has 265 books. How many books do they have altogether? Show your work. Explain what you did to solve the problem.

113. What is 441 – 377? Solve the problem and show how you got your answer.

114. Rita's Ribbon Shop sells ribbon by the centimeter. If Rita charges five cents for every centimeter, how much would this ribbon cost? Explain how you figured out the price.

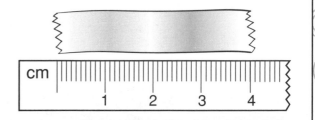

115. For one month the Robertson family and the Smith family kept track of the number of books they read. Which family read the most books? In which family did the mom read the most books? How do you know?

Robertson Family

Family Member	Books Read
Grandma	◁⩜
Mom	◁⩜ I
Jared	◁⩜ III
Ryan	IIII

Smith Family

Family Member	Books Read
Dad	III
Mom	◁⩜ II
Beth	◁⩜ IIII

©The Mailbox® • *Daily Math Prompts* • TEC61096

111.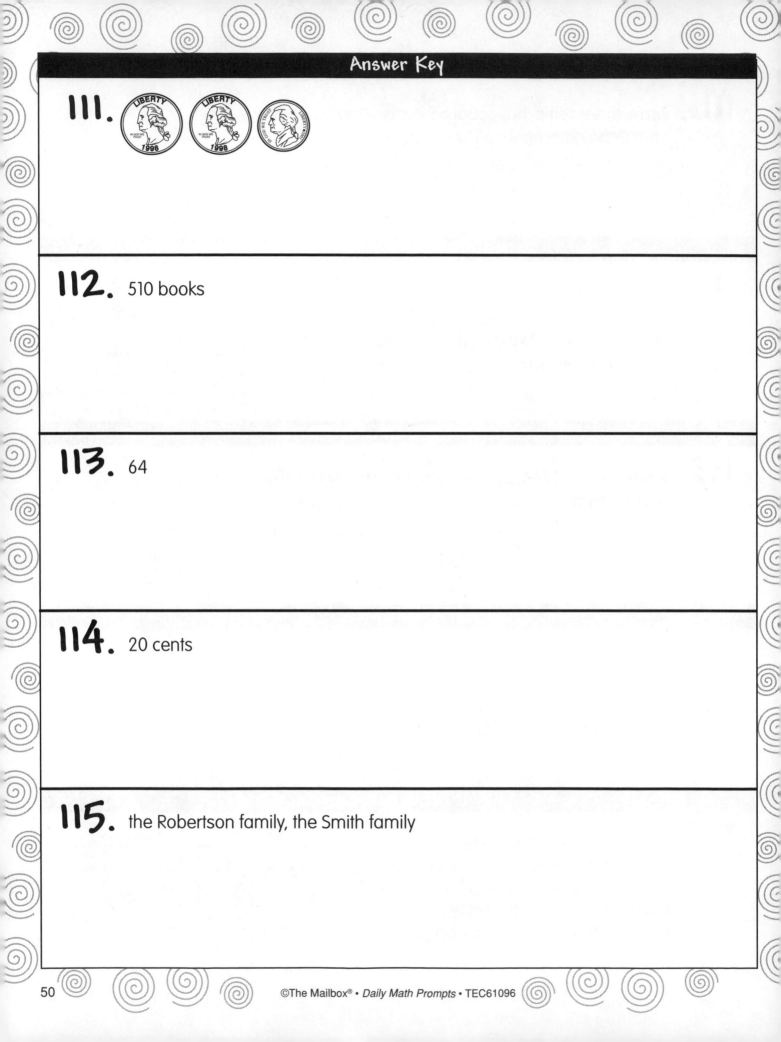

112. 510 books

113. 64

114. 20 cents

115. the Robertson family, the Smith family

NUMBER & OPERATIONS

116. Jon has $1.00. He buys an ice pop for 55¢. How much change should he get? Show how he could figure out the correct amount of change he is due.

NUMBER & OPERATIONS

117. Use the digits 1, 2, 3, 4, 5, and 6 to build the subtraction problem of three-digit numbers with the largest possible difference. Then build the subtraction problem of three-digit numbers with the smallest possible difference. Solve the problems. Show how you got your answers.

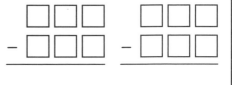

NUMBER & OPERATIONS

118. Dante wants to buy a muffin and a banana. How much money does he need? How did you find the answer?

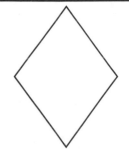

Breakfast Foods

Food		Cost
muffin		60¢
orange		25¢
cereal		62¢
banana		33¢

ALGEBRA

119. If ☆ = 8 and △ – ☆ = 16, what is the value of △?

GEOMETRY

120. Kendra wants to divide this shape into two congruent triangles. Draw the shape and then show her how to do this. How do you know that the shapes you drew are congruent?

116. 45¢

117.

6	5	4
−	1	2	3

    5   3   1

4	5	6
−	3	2	1

    1   3   5

118. 93¢

119. △ = 24

120.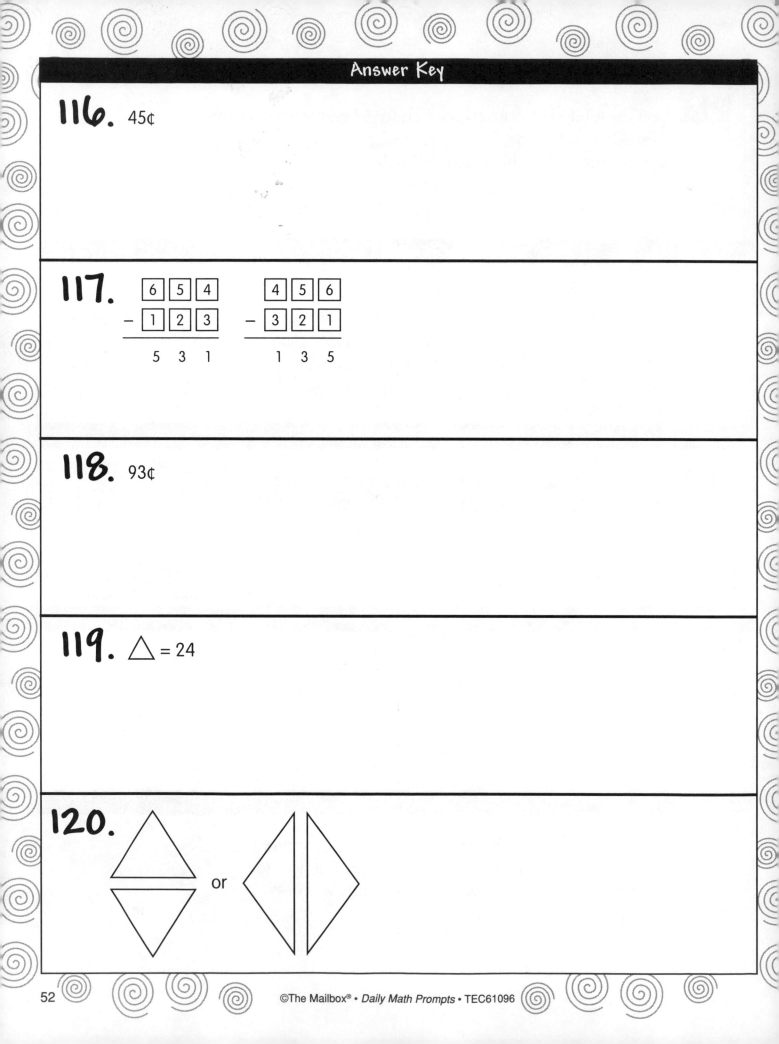

or

NUMBER & OPERATIONS

121. Which is worth more: 10 nickels or 8 dimes? How do you know?

NUMBER & OPERATIONS

122. The toy store sells a yo-yo for 60¢, a jump rope for 75¢, and a rubber ball for 25¢. Which costs more, the yo-yo or the ball? Which part of the problem is not needed to solve it? Why not?

NUMBER & OPERATIONS

123. Amy says that this cake is cut into equal parts. Is she right? Explain how you know.

ALGEBRA

124. Jane's book is 124 pages long. She reads 48 pages. How many more pages does she have left to read? Which number sentence can help you solve this problem? How do you know?

$124 - 48 = \boxed{}$

$124 + 48 = \boxed{}$

MEASUREMENT

125. Peter's backpack is 14 inches long. He says that 14 inches is the same as 1 foot and 3 inches. Is he correct? Why or why not?

121. 8 dimes

122. the yo-yo, that the jump rope costs 75¢

123. yes

124. 76, 124 – 48 = □

125. no

NUMBER & OPERATIONS

126. Show at least two different ways to show $1.00 using coins. Explain how you know each set of coins equals $1.00.

NUMBER & OPERATIONS

127. Chandra has 8 apples. She wants to put them into 4 equal groups. Show her how to do this. Then explain what you did.

NUMBER & OPERATIONS

128. Hunter put his dinosaurs in 5 rows of 4 dinosaurs each. How many dinosaurs does Hunter have? Draw a picture to solve this problem.

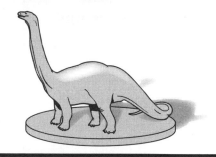

GEOMETRY

129. How is turning a shape different from flipping it? Explain your answer using pictures and words.

DATA ANALYSIS & PROBABILITY

130. Brenda needs to ask three questions that can be answered by collecting data. She writes the one shown. List two other questions that she could ask. Tell why each one is correct.

What are my classmates' favorite foods?

126. Answers will vary.

127.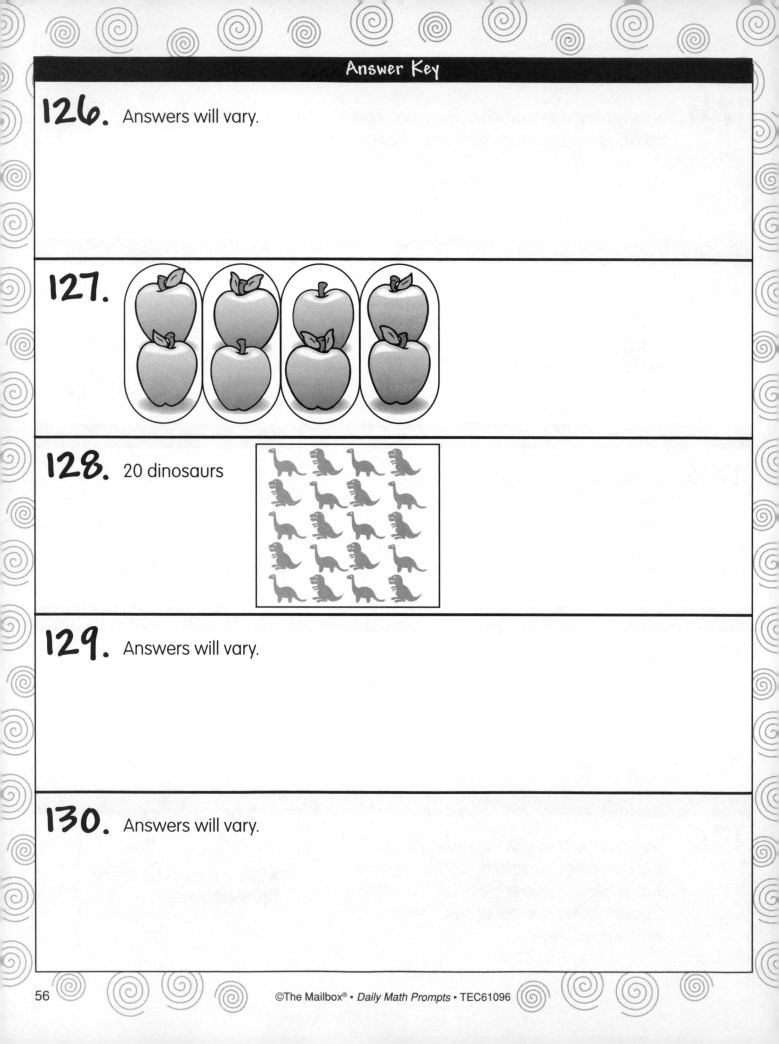

128. 20 dinosaurs

129. Answers will vary.

130. Answers will vary.

©The Mailbox® • *Daily Math Prompts* • TEC61096

NUMBER & OPERATIONS

131. Mindy has 35¢. She does not have any pennies. Show five different coin combinations she could have.

NUMBER & OPERATIONS

132. Keiko says that 2 x 4 = 4 x 2. Do you agree? Explain your thinking using numbers, pictures, or words.

NUMBER & OPERATIONS

133. Do you need to regroup to solve this subtraction problem? Explain how you know.

$$284 - 168$$

MEASUREMENT

134. Read the time on the clock. Randy says it is 25 minutes before four o'clock. Is he right? Explain your answer.

GEOMETRY

135. Make a list of at least three real-life objects that are cylinders.

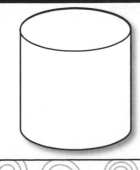

131.

132. yes

133. yes

134. no

135. Answers will vary.

NUMBER & OPERATIONS

136. How much money is this? Draw and label coins to show the same amount of money using fewer coins.

NUMBER & OPERATIONS

137. Nate has 4 baskets with 3 plums in each one. Write and solve an addition problem and a multiplication problem that show how many plums he has in all.

NUMBER & OPERATIONS

138. Cathy has 70¢ and wants to buy a toy. Look at the chart. List the toys she has enough money to buy. Explain your answers.

Toy Sale

Toy		Price
jump rope		75¢
ball		60¢
train		85¢
top		55¢

DATA ANALYSIS & PROBABILITY

139. How are a bar graph and a pictograph alike? How are they different? Use words, pictures, and numbers to explain your answers.

ALGEBRA

140. What is the value of △? Explain how you got your answer.

$$7 \times \triangle = 14$$

Answer Key

136. 70¢

137. 3 + 3 + 3 + 3 = 12 plums, 4 x 3 = 12 plums

138. ball and top

139. Answers will vary.

140. △ = 2

141. MaryAnn has three dollars, two quarters, two dimes, one nickel, and four pennies. How much money does she have in all? Show how you got your answer.

142. Isabella buys a pack of pencils for $3.46. She buys a binder for $4.12. How much does she spend in all? Explain how you got your answer.

143. Pam ate $\frac{1}{6}$ of the candy bar. Lila ate $\frac{3}{6}$ of the candy bar. Which girl ate more? How do you know?

144. How can J. R. flip this triangle? Draw a picture to show him how to do this. Then explain what you did.

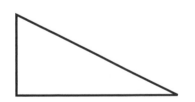

145. Lisa uses 3 apples to make one cup of applesauce. She uses 6 apples to make two cups of applesauce. She uses 9 apples to make three cups of applesauce. Complete the table to determine how many cups of applesauce she will make with 18 apples.

Apples	Cups of Applesauce
3	1
6	2
9	3
18	

141. $3.79

142. $7.58

143. Lila

144. Answers will vary.

145. 6 cups

Apples	Cups of Applesauce
3	1
6	2
9	3
12	4
15	5
18	6

NUMBER & OPERATIONS

146. Joshua has 75¢. If he buys a lollipop for 28¢ and a piece of gum for 25¢, how much will he have left? Show how you got your answer.

NUMBER & OPERATIONS

147. Tony cut his pizza into 10 equal parts. He ate 3 pieces of pizza. Write the fraction that shows the number of pieces he ate.

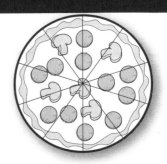

NUMBER & OPERATIONS

148. Show $3.85 using bills and coins. List, draw, and label your answer. Explain why your drawing is correct.

MEASUREMENT

149. Cory is measuring weight in grams and kilograms. Which is the best unit to use when weighing a pencil? Which is the best unit to use when weighing a bag of apples? Explain your answers.

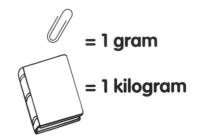

= 1 gram

= 1 kilogram

DATA ANALYSIS & PROBABILITY

150. Read the following events. Which one is certain? Which one is possible? Which one is impossible?

You will read from a book today.
The day after Monday will be Tuesday.
You will eat 1,000 hot dogs for lunch today.

146. 22¢

147. $\frac{3}{10}$ of the pieces

148. Answers will vary.

149. grams, kilograms

150. The day after Monday will be Tuesday.
You will read from a book today.
You will eat 1,000 hot dogs for lunch today.

NUMBER & OPERATIONS

151. Eric spent $1.95 on popcorn and $2.45 on a drink at the movies. How much did he spend in all? Show your work. Explain how you got your answer.

NUMBER & OPERATIONS

152. How much of the pie has been eaten? Explain how you know.

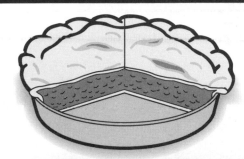

NUMBER & OPERATIONS

153. Beth has eight markers. Three are red. What fraction names the part of the markers that are not red? Show how you know.

ALGEBRA

154. Wes has 100 stamps. He gives 45 to his friend. He has 55 stamps left. Write a number sentence to match the story. Tell how you knew what to write.

GEOMETRY

155. Sharon's teacher asked her to draw a cube on the board. Look at what she drew. Is she correct? Explain why or why not.

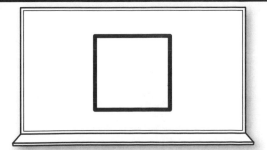

151. $4.40

152. $\frac{1}{3}$ of the pie

153. $\frac{5}{8}$ of the markers

154. $100 - 45 = 55$ stamps

155. no

NUMBER & OPERATIONS

156. Look at Molly's toys. What fraction of her toys are dolls? What fraction are balls? How did you figure out the fractions?

NUMBER & OPERATIONS

157. Gerri is walking 4 dogs. Each dog has 2 ribbons in its fur. How many ribbons are there in all? Explain how you got your answer.

NUMBER & OPERATIONS

158. Luis has 12 peaches and 4 bags. If he puts the same number of peaches in each bag, what fraction of the peaches are in each bag? Use numbers, pictures, and words to explain your thinking.

MEASUREMENT

159. Look at the tools. Which would you use to measure flour while baking cookies? Which could you use to measure your desk? Which tool could you use to measure the temperature outside? Which one could you use to weigh an apple?

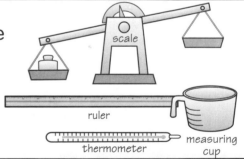

ALGEBRA

160. Write the next three numbers in the pattern. What is the rule for the pattern? How do you know?

2, 7, 12, 17, 22, ___, ___, ___

156. $\frac{7}{15}$ of the toys, $\frac{8}{15}$ of the toys

157. 8 ribbons

158. $\frac{3}{12}$ of the peaches

159. measuring cup, ruler, thermometer, scale

160. 27, 32, 37; add 5

161. Mary had $5.00. She bought a burger for $3.95. How much money does she have now? Explain how you got your answer.

162. Pete needs to solve 5 x 6. Show and tell him two different ways he could find the answer.

163. Anton has 10 pencils. Three of the pencils are black and seven are red. What fraction of the pencils are red? How did you get your answer?

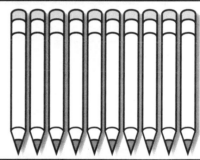

164. Allison has 2 red shirts, 3 black shirts, 2 brown shirts, and 1 blue shirt in her bag. If she grabs a shirt without looking, which color shirt is she most likely to pick? Which color shirt is she least likely to pick? Which colors would she be equally likely to pick? Explain your answers.

165. Which of these figures have at least five faces? Tell how you know.

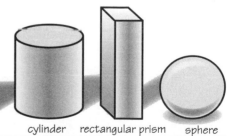

cone   cube   cylinder   rectangular prism   sphere

161. $1.05

162. Answers will vary.

163. $\frac{7}{10}$ of the pencils

164. black, blue, red and brown

165. cube and rectangular prism

NUMBER & OPERATIONS

166. Tanner planted 3 rows of flowers in his garden, with 5 flowers in each row. Write a multiplication problem to find out how many flowers he planted in all. How did you know what to write?

NUMBER & OPERATIONS

167. Will has 9 toy cars. $\frac{4}{9}$ of the toy cars are blue and $\frac{5}{9}$ of the toy cars are green. Does Will have more blue or green toy cars? How do you know?

NUMBER & OPERATIONS

168. Bree cut her loaf of bread into 8 equal slices. She made a sandwich with 2 of the slices. What fraction of the bread is left? Explain how you got your answer.

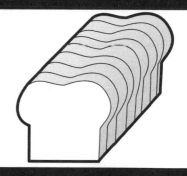

MEASUREMENT

169. Read the thermometer. What is the temperature? Is it a good day to build a snowman? Explain your answer.

DATA ANALYSIS & PROBABILITY

170. What number is the spinner most likely to land on? What number is it least likely to land on? How do you know?

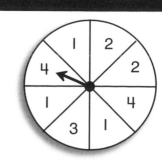

166. $3 \times 5 = 15$ flowers

167. green toy cars

168. $\frac{6}{8}$ of the bread

169. 85°, no

170. 1, 3

NUMBER & OPERATIONS

171. Shawn has 16 bananas. He wants to put them into groups of 3. How many groups can he make? Will he have any bananas left over? Explain how you got your answers.

NUMBER & OPERATIONS

172. I am a three-digit number. The digit in my hundreds place is 3 less than the digit in my tens place. The digit in my tens place is 2 more than the digit in my ones place. The digit in my ones place is 6. What number am I? Explain how you got your answer.

___ ___ ___

NUMBER & OPERATIONS

173. Write these numbers in order from greatest to least. How do you know this order is correct?

357, 218, 298, 375

ALGEBRA

174. Ben, Toby, Mel, and Andre are standing in line. Mel is third in line. Toby is behind Andre and in front of Mel. Ben is last in line. Who is first in line? Explain how you know.

MEASUREMENT

175. There are 4 quarts in 1 gallon. How many quarts are in 3 gallons? Explain how you figured out the answer.

171. 5 groups, yes

172. 586

173. 375, 357, 298, 218

174. Andre (The correct order is Andre, Toby, Mel, Ben.)

175. 12 quarts

NUMBER & OPERATIONS

176. Solve the number sentence. Then write a story problem to match it.

$$2 \times 4 = \boxed{}$$

NUMBER & OPERATIONS

177. There are 8 pieces of candy. Angie gives 2 pieces of candy to each of her friends. How many friends does she give candy to? Show and explain how you found your answer.

NUMBER & OPERATIONS

178. Each student must have a partner for the field trip. There are 26 students in Class A, 28 students in Class B, and 30 students in Class C. Can each student have a classmate as a partner? Explain why or why not.

Class A	26
Class B	28
Class C	30

GEOMETRY

179. How is a cone different from a pyramid?

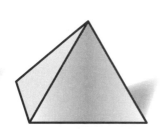

DATA ANALYSIS & PROBABILITY

180. If Danny spins the spinner, which color is the spinner most likely to land on? Which color is least likely? Explain your thinking.

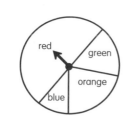

176. 8; Answers will vary.

177. 4 friends

178. yes

179. Answers will vary.

180. red, blue

Math Prompt Checklist

Use this handy checklist to help you keep track of each prompt used throughout the year.

✓	Prompt	✓	Prompt	✓	Prompt	✓	Prompt	✓	Prompt	✓	Prompt
	1		31		61		91		121		151
	2		32		62		92		122		152
	3		33		63		93		123		153
	4		34		64		94		124		154
	5		35		65		95		125		155
	6		36		66		96		126		156
	7		37		67		97		127		157
	8		38		68		98		128		158
	9		39		69		99		129		159
	10		40		70		100		130		160
	11		41		71		101		131		161
	12		42		72		102		132		162
	13		43		73		103		133		163
	14		44		74		104		134		164
	15		45		75		105		135		165
	16		46		76		106		136		166
	17		47		77		107		137		167
	18		48		78		108		138		168
	19		49		79		109		139		169
	20		50		80		110		140		170
	21		51		81		111		141		171
	22		52		82		112		142		172
	23		53		83		113		143		173
	24		54		84		114		144		174
	25		55		85		115		145		175
	26		56		86		116		146		176
	27		57		87		117		147		177
	28		58		88		118		148		178
	29		59		89		119		149		179
	30		60		90		120		150		180

Assessment

Student: _____   Date: _____

Prompt: _____   Skill: _____

Answer:

☐ Correct answer
☐ Partial answer, wrong problem, or computation error
☐ Incorrect or no answer

Understanding:

☐ Understands the math needed
☐ Understands most of the math needed
☐ Understands little of the math needed

Written explanation:

☐ Communicates idea clearly
☐ Communicates idea fairly well
☐ Communicates idea poorly

Comments: _____

_____

_____

_____

_____

_____

©The Mailbox® • *Daily Math Prompts* • TEC61096

Assessment

Student: _____   Date: _____

Prompt: _____   Skill: _____

Answer:

☐ Correct answer
☐ Partial answer, wrong problem, or computation error
☐ Incorrect or no answer

Understanding:

☐ Understands the math needed
☐ Understands most of the math needed
☐ Understands little of the math needed

Written explanation:

☐ Communicates idea clearly
☐ Communicates idea fairly well
☐ Communicates idea poorly

Comments: _____

_____

_____

_____

_____

_____

©The Mailbox® • *Daily Math Prompts* • TEC61096

_____'s

Journal

$14 + 12 = 26$

Prompt Number: ____________ Date: ________________

____

____

Prompt Number: ____________ Date: ________________

____

____

©The Mailbox® • *Daily Math Prompts* • TEC61096